Lust, Love, & Loss

By: Mystkue

Forward by Antoine RJ Wright

For more information, visit Mystkue at : www.mystkue.com

ISBN 978-1-68411-526-6

90000

9 781684 115266

Poet's Remarks...

My words are my life line as my experiences fuel the blood in my veins. For every word, I wrote in this book is based off of an experience. Over the years I have seen so many relationships affected by the conundrum of Lust, Love, and Loss. I believe that regardless of what kind of relationship an individual has with another person or even within themselves at some point they experience at least two of these feelings. Each feeling creates a moment in time that shapes our experiences as humans and what drives our perception in both positive and negative ways.

I encourage you as you read to take time and reflect on your experiences. My poetry is set to provoke your nerve and address topics you only think about in your inner thoughts or write about in your journal. I want you to smile, cry, laugh, and scream as you use this chapbook to ignite those feelings you swear you have moved on from. Question your heart, question your mind, ask yourself "if I was in this situation again would I make the same choice.?"

Within this book, I have provided questions, author's purpose behind pieces, as well as an area for you to record your thoughts. My goal is to impact, inspire, and influence you to go on this journey of Lust, Love, and Loss. Reminisce on the good times and take away lessons from the not so great ones. Relish in your truth and unapologetically feel whatever emotion you need to feel! Feel empowered to share your thoughts with me on all my social networks. Join the Mystkue movement!

Remember,
Your Petal is Your Legacy! I hope you enjoy!

Unforgettably Yours,

Mystkue

Foreword

By: Antoine RJ Wright

Temperance causes temperatures warning of tickled catastrophes
Revealing words degreed like celebrities at the infancies of Celsius
Or was it hurt by fairies heightened off
Fahrenheit's imperial apostrophes
Nevertheless, the grammar stammered along until it became an
inescapable reality
These merely the teary leaves left for pleading something other than
insanity
These leaves plead with your abilities to perceive heart's need
To believe once deceived
Pocket between eyelids inescapable dreams
Then rocket into emotional soliloquies at the measure of Mystkue

It's probably appropriate to level a forward which compliments the at-
tention and talents of Mystkue but also arrives at it in a similar fashion.
Mystkue's temperament is so very present in each of her pieces. Each
time I read, there was this warning of emotions to be tickled — hap-
piness and sadness, sensuality and indifference. Her wordplay offers
something of a temperature gauge to the life of others who have found
themselves growing up in a time where the imagination and reality of
kingdoms of the mind and heart are fostered and challenged.

Where it seems many prose writers struggle with grammar, poetic
license taken by Mystkue offers a different — and better — reality.
You read along the line breaks and find one set of emotions, you read
along where your breath breaks and find yet another. It is a bit of play

with some sensibilities, and then you see re-pattern and her words open skillfully and artistically. You find some pieces leaving your heart yearning for more, but it's yours, hers has been satisfied in the words and line breaks. You believe hers and realize that yours is also a part of Mystkue's journey.

Here's where it might make sense to hear what pieces motivated such comments. Yet, we won't paint your perspective with that kind of foreshadowing. When reading Mystkue's prose, you'll find some pieces shining brighter at some moments, as others come alive for you in others. You might find a few deeper than your sensibilities, and a few abbreviated — a distinct want on your part for more from the pen. This is what makes this collection so interesting; you aren't going to merely appreciate the pieces. You'll appreciate the entirety. It's the collective life experiences of Mystkue best found — it's the separate snapshots we are given insight to in each piece which shines.

So, read Mystkue's prose with eyes open, with your journey also open. Allow her to take you into her heart's intricacies and fallacies. Then, when you've completed in whole or in part, find yourself responding to the soliloquies in your own heart. Take a picture or scribble a few lines. But, don't measure yours against hers. Mystkue's prose represents her measuring stick only. But you can learn from her openness, her rhythm, and her growth. This is what this collection offers. And like myself, I hope you find yourself nudged into appreciating the journey, not just the destination.

The Journey

In the beginning, you seek to look for what appeals to you and you begin to Lust…

Before you've taken the voyage to understand what has been sought and its purpose, you've fallen in Love…

As you recollect memories and recuperate physically, mentally, and emotionally, you find that you are no longer whole; fatally incomplete. You have experienced Loss…

Lust

Palms sweat when we… as our bodies intertwined, letting the stress from our crowded days unwind. We are who we are separately but like magnets we attract naturally. Sometimes we take on the dare of exploring the unknown because we can't keep our feelings intact.

The desire to want someone or something is so innate that it can be mind boggling and as mystifying as trying to solve a jigsaw puzzle. How we interact with these individuals and desire something we can't physically touch is like kinetic chemistry shooting through our veins. We want SATISFACTION. This yearning causes us to make spontaneous decisions. Some of which we regret later on during reflection.

Lust complicates things as it can be a catalyst to falling head over heels early on or a barrier that prevents one from thorough expression. Lust is our inner fantasies, those that are hidden in the subconscious. Mostly created by our desire of physical attraction but can extrapolate our dreams and worst nightmares. Lust stimulates us to challenge our psyche.

An even balance of an overdose of dopamine and serotonin. Easily manipulating us to become imprisoned as addicts.

Careful, lust can be a sense of entitlement or greediness. Take heed and try to contain your composure. Not everything is meant for us to have in the immediate moment. Most things are received best in doses.

Remember,

Lust is tricky, a chameleon of emotions consistently overlapping in change. The one thing we want the most can be the most detrimental to us or it can be a blessing.

Lust is the gift and the curse.

Unforgettably yours,

Mystkue

Lust, Love, Loss

Table of Contents

"Stung by Cupid"

She said,
You gave me chlamydia.
Yet She still ain't get rid of ya.
And I bet all of y'all would call
her stupid.
Like y'all ain't never been stung
by Cupid.

Who said she was not hurting
inside?
Cause he denied her for his
pride.
He needed somebody to blame.
So, he deflected hate and disgust.
Leaving her to cope alone.
Like she already wasn't ashamed.

A fucked-up circumstance.
From a four-word statement-
She could've withheld, popped
the pills -
Moved on.
But those actions would be too
blatant.

Or would y'all blame it on her
being ashamed?
If she kept quiet,

Although it's not in her to be
dishonest.
This shit just sat on her conscious.

To speak up or be silent.
To be silent or speak up?
Either way.

A fucked-up circumstance,
Like this -
Would cause-

Mistrust.
But who would y'all say was in the
wrong?
When on many nights,
Both parties lost countless battles
to
Lust.

So yes, she stayed.
And they dealt with it.
Together they prayed.
For a plan to restore.
And I bet y'all would call them
stupid.
Like y'all ain't never been stung by
Cupid.

Lust, Love, Loss

"BDSM"

In the moment, I was in calming shock.
My eyes blinded and closed shut.
I tried to visualize the roses -
The candlelight,
Your shadow flickering in the light.

I inhaled your pheromones
Your cologne danced on my nostril hairs,
As I-
Tuned into the tempo
My veins pulsated possessively.
Sighs and Deep moans.

I couldn't think straight, wondering what-
Was being done to me
You refocused my senses to ignore my self-consciousness.
You explored my many curves .

I'd forgotten
Where I was
Your touch soothed yet applied just the right-
Pressure.
Cotton and silk tightened against my skin-
My insides contracted,
Boosted my experience.
Sighs and Deep moans-
Pleasure.

Lust, Love, Loss

"Kaleidoscope"

Thoughts of you,
Cascaded-
My mind like a kaleidoscope of pictures.
Reds, yellows, and surely royal blue
Pigments of color -
Sculpted murals of you!

Swirling around in my memoir
A fairytale from noir and blanc
To-
The vibrantly hued saga
Of me and you.

Attempted to follow the patterns
Encrypted amid the image
Many with-voluminous meanings
I'd uncover your greatness, like we were inseparable variables
Watching you formulate, code, and solve for the perfect remedy.

A solution to elaborate equations;
Behind the beauty of light and eclipse.
A tableau with a powerful message
Like the history of NASA and Hidden Figures
A kaleidoscope of pictures
Cascaded-
My mind,
With reds, yellows, and surely royal blue
Thoughts of…
Me and you!

Lust, Love, Loss

"The ACT"

Tantalized by the sensation of the friction,
Between-
Our Twisted Blend.
Mahogany, chestnut, sprinkles of praline-
Fellatio is so sensual, here lies a skill-set mean.
Yes! I said it. I became a fiend.
Coupled with hot and foggy showers,
Bathing off sins.
After six or more climaxes,
Leaving countless grins.
Now cleansed.
The melody of lust.
We feel as we cross-pollinate,
During mass episodes when we congregate.
Our bodies tangle as we copulate.
Such mannerisms, we possessed
That first allowed us to trust.

"Inebriation"

Cigar smoke
Cloudy haze
Dazed and confused
How it flurries

Keeps those wise guys
Amused
Blowing smoke just sets the mood
It was with the tone of a challenge

"Sweat"

You really swept a girl off her feet.
Now you in need of a towel,
'Cause you drenched from how she sweatin' you.
Maybe if you would've just fucked!
And didn't give her a glimpse,
Of how you treat your women with a crown-
She wouldn't be in love with you.
Yearning for you.
Waiting for you.
Maybe even a lil' bit of begging and pleading for you
Her face would still be in a frown.
You wouldn't be drenched in all that-
Sweat

"Lifeguard"

Guard me with your stature!
To which the electricity strikes, like a match-
To the hairs on my skin.
Help me develop life, within.

Feed my soul with coercion.
As your eyes fool me,
And your touch takes me on a physical excursion.

Save me life guard!

Rescue me from 12-foot waves,
To which you make me twitch;
As your tongue flicks my switch.
Revive me in ways,
To which I succumb to a threesome.

Save me life guard!

Submerge in my dreams,
Like a submarine.
Apply pressure to withhold my screams

Save me life guard!

Swallow me and make me angst.
Swaddle me with your strength.
Investigate me thoroughly with your length.

Save me life guard!

Til' the sunrise glistens,
Over a magnificent view.
The coalescence of me and you.

Life guard, save me!

Lust, Love, Loss

"If I was a Bird"

I'd fly afar reminiscent of birds
Bravery soaring depths and ferocious heights
Embodying courage of strength by wingspan
Observing perspectives shedding luminescence: freedom, paradigms
Bridging pathways between God and Us
Gliding by carrying wisdom of life.

"Prepare me"

I've heard you answer many times before.
When I was broken,
Or riding on a high horse.
But in this instance-
You have yet to answer.
I'm beginning to feel ignored.

What is it, you are preparing me for?
Haven't I proven my willingness?
Sown the seeds,
Watered them,
Watched them flourish,
Plucked petals and thorns?

What about the appearance you foresee?
I'm telling you, without them I'm incomplete.
Do I contest or compete with your destiny for me?

I can dress to impress-
Even deflect to relieve my stress.
But tell me God,
What is it, you are preparing me for?

Is it to accept the purity of me?
Within my nudity,
The agility to bare my soul
With your Support of making me whole
First without them-
Is it for you to allow me to see the beauty in me?

Lust, Love, Loss

Who is them, you ask?
From a promise vowed-
Forming one union.
Sickness and health
Even simple mistakes, because we're human.

The greatest manifestation-
A spirit that bores within me.
A blessing growing in my womb.

Oh tell me God, what are you preparing me for?

"Wo-man"

Vagina monologue forces dialogue amongst men
Intricately sewn creation from his ribcage
Being part of him doesn't equate entrapment
Let her fly, explore the sky
Experience joy, pain, sunshine, and rain
The beautiful solution to recreation, woman

Lust, Love, Loss

"Push"

This talent is like vomit
It comes so consistently consistent in its consistency.
Well, let you tell it this is who
I'm meant to be
You see,
Do you really know what it's like to be a struggling artist?
These things are not done for char-i-ty
How you get to gloat and feel transformed
Off my stress
Sending accolades through text
Like
"Mystkue I'm Impressed"

That's great on your end
But for me
I'm struggling to see the light
Hoping that this talent soars
And in return pays for my flight

Don't get me wrong, I'm blessed!
That you, you, and you.
See potential.
That's all the more reason why I stress!

I'm out here trying to make a way
Not for anybody else
But just to be my best

So, I'm hoping that this talent

Lust, Love, Loss

Stays limitless like time

See without it
I'm no good
I gotta succeed
The desire to BE
Is consistently consistent in its consistency.

So i guess ill continue on this road and PUSH...

Author's Thoughts

Writing these poems, took place during a time when I was coming into myself. As I wrote, I reflected how I felt directly after I graduated from college and I needed to find myself. I chose lust because most think of the ordinary definition, but I find that I lust after my dreams, wants, and desires as well. My favorite poem in the lust series is "Prepare Me." As a woman, I am always striving to be my best self so I can be ready for what God has in store for me. Lust is a powerful agent, oftentimes making just as much as an effort to your memories as it did in the moment it was sparked. How are you allowing lust to be felt, but not drive your ways forward?

YOUR LEGACY

_____
_____
_____
_____
_____
_____
_____
_____
_____
_____
_____
_____
_____
_____
_____

YOUR LEGACY CONTINUED...
Lust, Love, Loss

_____

_____

_____

_____

_____

_____

_____

_____

_____

_____

_____

_____

_____

_____

_____

_____

_____

_____

_____

_____

_____

_____

_____

_____

_____

YOUR LEGACY CONTINUED…

Lust, Love, Loss

"Fig"

We sat awkwardly, vibing graciously-
To the music.
As the floor vibrated beneath us,
I studied you immensely.
Wondering if you could feel me staring so intensely.
I...
Underestimated the moments thereafter,
A few head nods, elongated eye fuckery, and soul laughter
Our worlds tangled.
I...
Continued to let the night slip by
As you kissed me with chivalry
This was one the first of hopefully
Many
By the end, we were so wrapped up in one another
Sitting gracefully, vibing flirtatiously
To the music
As the floor vibrated beneath us

...

One week had passed
And you still hadn't asked me for any ass
Yet our paths seemed to keep
Weaving
Like baskets
I...
Wanted to fill yours
With memories and soliloquies
Of the time we shared together
Your kiss remained noble
I....
Dived into your mental
Just to pass time..
As we sat awkwardly, vibing graciously

To the music...

"Ride"

This rollercoaster ride-
Thrills.
Up, down, round, and round
Applies pressure
Dismantling weight
Slams and jams,
Kills.
Awakes a roar in you
You didn't notice that he can feel it too
Screams and let's not forget cream
Your neighbors,
They hear you boo!
A ride of a lifetime.
Moving faster than the speed of light
Shivers and quivers
A bath in the forsaken
River
Pressure subsides
Weight dissipates
Leaving behind
Debris from explosions.
No time to take cover
Showers of turmoil
Hide.
Oh, how remarkable,
Was your turn
On his rollercoaster ride?

Lust, Love, Loss

"Nausea"

When my breath creates waves from my rib cage I become,
Invincible
Like I've swallowed kryptonite
Every ounce of me begins to collapse,
Into-
The sheets.
A chill creeps,
Up my inner thigh
Circling the tip of the Mountain top
He has
Found his way!
His way
Sends shivers
Through my river stream
As my blood rushes
I feel
Nauseous

"Robert Sylvester"

Robert Sylvester
Does he tickle your fantasy?
Gushy moist and juicy-

All that in your panties.

Sweet rhythmic tunes
Baby take off your clothes
Skin so smooth
The color of sand dunes

Robert Sylvester
The sensual investor
The theory of relativity to
Your physical phenomenon
Booty
Lips
Hips
Thighs
Something like Einstein

The catalyst to your climax
Dick
A mind of its own
Genius
You know he loves it when you lick-
Sugary substances from the
Tip

Lust, Love, Loss

Sweet rhythmic tunes
His delight
That honey love
Spread your legs apart
As he proceeds to go low
His tongue fluttering your heart

Do you follow his flow
Get up on a room
Hurricane
Blow
Boom

Robert Sylvester
Does he tickle your fantasy
Gushy moist and juicy

All that in your panties

"*Licorice*"
Like licorice on my lips
Ushering chills down my spine
Sensually seducing me
Tantalizing tales of lovers quarrel

Lust, Love, Loss

"Busy Bee"

Simply enough I just wanted him to continue on as a busy bee
Fondling and playing all in my honey jar
Making me his queen
Fantasizing I was better than his favorite porn star
Keeping me sticky and sweet mostly moist filled with cream
I wanted him to lick
Better yet suck on me
Until my skin melted
In his mouth
Like ice
Watching my nipples shiver
As he looked me into my eyes
Playing with my honey comb
My legs quivered
Continuously acting as the director
Never saying cut
Simply since 3-4 hours
Of a love making scene
Wouldn't suffice
Immersed in his curse
My thighs pierced
And
Tingled
As he submerged in my honey jar
Oooh
What a little busy bee

Lust, Love, Loss

"Slope"

We fucked until we both exploded
Our crevices creased repeatedly over
Several inclines
I tried to solve for y.
And you for x.
These moments we created,
As we colored-
In and out,
Out and in,
With each stroke going deeper
You pulled me closer
Our breaths in sync
We were coloring
Outside the lines
Each thrust resulted in the rise of my hips
Screams of pleasure
Inversely proportional to you gripping my waist
Securing me against running from
Your dick.
You scooped me like a spoon fulfilling each curve
This is the tale of how you became one of the twelve Olympians
My Michael Phelps
You had me as you mastered the backstroke
8 medals in
I gulp, swallowed, mmm,
That good ole' deep throat

As you solved for x and me for y.

"Things Feel Better in Cramped Spaces"

Things feel better in cramped spaces.
Like directing films-
Cutting right to the chase.
Positioning every part in place

Painting blindly with imagery.
The moisture fogs the windows
Leaving visuals impaired
Heat rises in cramped spaces.

Touch guides familiarity in cramped places.
Caressing all seams intricately woven.
Murmurs sound like lullabies
Mimicking MJ's Butterflies

Sculpting bodies in motion
Like breaths racing marathons
Braking once climax is reached
Revelations taking us to new destinations.

Lust, Love, Loss

"The Many Men I've slept with"

Let's start with the ex
Hmm yeah soft sensual touch
That made me cum by a caress
My body succumbed to him
Like a mammal adapting to the seasons
We reversed roles as I
Forever
Held the key to his lock

Then there was the first
Who brought my love parts to life
I learned the anatomy of me
Experimentally
That's the way love goes

Had me caught way up in his rapture
Enough to allow the moisture to escape him and
Rest on the tip of my lips
Sun kissed by the rays
He'd have my clit throbbing for days
The first to dive in
Below 20 feet deep

Then it was that one
Who taught me the art of a moan
Damn I should have never left him alone.

This is just the beginning of many stories to be told

Oh, the many men, I've slept with
To be continued...

Lust, Love, Loss

Lust, Love, Loss

Love

Love is something in the depths of our souls we yearn for. It is the oxygen that keeps us alive. Its decadence is intangible. Love is experiences. Love is pain. Love is happiness. Love is fear. Love is anxiety. Love is loyalty.

What is it about this simple yet complex word that has us in situations that have us uncomfortable and questioning the fibers of our very being?

Love is powerful in its purest form. Simply magical. The smiles that it brings to those who feel it, gives hope to others. Us millennials call it #relationshipgoals.

As I disseminated these pieces, I chose to divulge the aesthetic of love from varied perspectives to convey how it bounds us as people. Every bond matters.

From the things that make us smile to even the things that make us cry. This love section will take us through what it's like to relish in our own emotions and simultaneously experience that same love from another vantage point.

Let's uncover emotions we never knew existed.

Remember,

Love is everything and nothing at the same time. it is up to you where you stand.

Unforgettably yours,

Mystkue

Table of Contents

"Prayer"

I'm begging!
What do I have to do Lord?
To be, someone's
Wife

I know you preparing them
And you going to bring him
When I'm ready.
But how long must I wait?

This life is treacherous
Devils I can't escape
I'm coming to you, Lord God
Pleading
Asking for you
To descend my only
Hope for purpose

To be his backbone
And bear his child

I know you have a lesson
You want me to learn
But can't you see
A family
Of my own is what I
Yearn?

Help me to understand,

The things that are not clear.
For I know you love all your children.
But sometimes God,
It seems my prayers go unheard.
Or that may just be my fear!

I ask that you make things clear
Show me how I can
Become a better woman
So that when he arrives
To stand by my side
To honor and protect
I grasp his hand
With no regrets

We will call unto you
To be our witness
When we say
I DO

"Homeless"

I'd slit my wrist a thousand times
To shed blood
And
Rebirth
Your lifeline

I'd cry a body of water
To replenish you
From your drought
Pushing you to keep swimming
Even though you want out

I'd climb 8,850 meters to the peak
To watch the sun
Irradiate you
As you grin

Unveiling the dimple, in your cheek

I'd twirl indefinitely
To stir up dark clouds
Concealing you from your enemies

I'd wipe the strait
Formed down your face
As you yell your pain aloud

I'd tell you the illness
That once tested your faith
Can't consume your brilliance
And mistakes

Yours and even mine
Sometimes force us to break
Then-
Rebuild

Our mistakes though, are not meant for us to have eternal stillness

I'd slit my wrist a thousand times
To convey strength
For each wound
Carries moral to the story

I'd walk with you hand in hand
The Ossie to your Ruby
To reclaim the message, you wanted translated

I'd scribble countlessly on this dear notepad
Until yours, mine, hers, and his pain
Was legible enough to be voiced
Til generations long after us
Couldn't feel forced to be ashamed
And knew they had a choice

I'd slit my wrist a thousand times
To shed blood
And
Rebirth
Your lifeline

To be HEARD
And

HEALED

"Kinesthetically Inclined"

As thoughts traveled
We once intersected
Souls COMBINED
Our pulses rumbled
We'd sway during walks, kicking gravel
I gazed at you as if you were my reflection
Souls DEFINED
We   were   grateful.
To one another
T I M E   S P E N T
Manifesting as lovers
Souls combined
Souls defined
We'd sway during walks, kicking gravel
As thoughts
T R A V E L E D...
We once Intersected
I gazed at you as if you were my reflection
Kinesthetically inclined

"HIM"

Lone wolf

Melanin pigmented

Masculine rush

Hair coils of a rich soil

Textured skin

Battered by life

Still smooth

Bass tunes

Of a harmonious blues

Baritone

Rugged cathartic touch

Humbled

Gaping sight

By rumination

Lust, Love, Loss

"21"

Number 21
North and south magnets
A pair like no other. That one. He who gets under
Skin
The skin you're in
In all the right ways

North and south magnets
A pair like no other,
And
Challenge you to become...

A single Sunflower,
In a field of grass...Just so he can
Admire.
Flourish.
Grow-
You
Embarking on a journey...
Together
In all the right ways--Now that's something
Worthy

Number 21?
Can you feel me
Purely
Can you feel

North and south magnets
A pair like no other,
Smiling because

We are now one

Lust, Love, Loss

"My Forever"

When we said that-

Did we know it would be another 99 years until we crossed paths
again?

From that time, I sat in your shadow as I watched you blossom

Warming those around you

Creating daylight

You had helped me flourished through the night

52,689,027.9 minutes spent honoring our union

My kindred spirit shining so bright

From afar

We made a vow

To evolve within ourselves

As a unit

Which brings us to this moment right now

When you will watch me glean from your light

For just a short moment

When we can bask in our sentiments

Embracing one another

Honoring this path

That you and I

We

Chose as lovers

Hold steady

Take flight

"Im Mense"

The sensuality of a forehead kiss made me coo like a dove.
Tantalizing smell of him extrapolated my senses,
Heightening my awareness.
His intellect intriguingly able to mind fuck my brain as I
Imagined unraveling the seams.
The innovation sparked from an idea with depth matured over time.
As thoughts left me memorized by my memories until next time.

"Knight"

His stature stood tall and firm as he was her soldier
He was there to guide, honor, and protect her
She didn't have to ask much as he exceeded her expectations
She yearned for him
His intellect stimulated her
He was her motivation
It's like he knew her down to a science
She was his one and only computation
Crazy thing is they never saw it coming
Both ignored the little birds humming
She'd gaze at his stature as he stood tall
He knew she was something real delicate yet firm
He yearned for her long term
She would follow, honor, and defend him
As he didn't have to ask much because she ignited
The fuel to his fire

Lust, Love, Loss

"Humble"

Why am I not the humblest poet?
You see it takes courage to say the least
The only way you become humble
Listen to the gossip folks mumble
Then go silent
Their rumors will start to crumble
'Cause they've realized you've tackled
Your fears
But yet,
They say I'm still not humble
I beg to differ because I marvel at these artists
Hoping that my spirit is the stewardess
To a healthy harvest
Of unlimited rhymes that tell a story about
These miraculous societies
Energizing cultural varieties
All to-
Engage
Empower
Endorse
One humanity
I want to be the vocal campaign
Just like the aspirations of my counterparts
I strive to encourage unity

So why am I not the humblest poet
You see it takes courage to say the least
The only way to become humble

Endorse

Empower

Continue to build my empire

It all takes hope, perseverance, courage to say the least

To become a humble lyricist, telling the story

As an activist

Synergizing cultural varieties

Within miraculous societies

Its the humility in me to be the

HUMBLEST.

"Monarchs"

Butterflies rang out as you approached me.
Inside I was-
Jumping for joy and smiling from ear to ear.
I played it cool.
For fear if I exposed my excitement, I'd look like a fool.
You gestured so subtly to inform me that you were in charge.
Releasing my composure to freedom-
With you, I escaped into moments of happiness.
Thoroughly full of innocence and laughter.
Staring into the depth of your crystal russet eyes-
To a world of fun and friendly competition.
Yet you still managed to regain control by randomly challenging,
My intuition!
Encouraging me with yes you can,
Good jobs, and in due time
Leading me to see you -
Indeed, I saw you
And you and me
Which crossed my mind as
Us
Damn it was just the first date and you gave me
Butterflies

Lust, Love, Loss

Author's Thoughts

Love, I must say is the thing I yearn for most but simultaneously most afraid of. It is definitely like a drug that consumes me, and I am consistently challenged yet fulfilled by the potential of the mere feeling. My favorite poem in the love series is "ImMense." This poem chronologizes exactly how I react to any entity of love. It's brief but it encompasses the mental, spiritual, emotional, and physicality affect love creates. Love finds itself as much as we find it, in a place where you were found by love, how did you respond? How will you respond if love finds you again?

YOUR LEGACY

_____

_____

_____

_____

_____

_____

_____

_____

_____

_____

_____

_____

_____

_____

_____

_____

YOUR LEGACY CONTINUED...

Lust, Love, Loss

YOUR LEGACY CONTINUED...

"Love Subdued Blues"

As I lay in your T-shirt
Your scent teases my senses
It calms me in a way that I've never felt before
My breaths slow down
The hairs on my neck rise
And I start to fantasize
Once upon a time
His hand caressed mine
We'd sway, boogie, and frolic
To the sultry sounds of Miles, Ella, Duke, and Nina
Bellowed laughter from deep within-
We walked hand and hand under navy skies
Laid in hammocks, rested in one another arms
Listened to the leaves rustle and bluebirds cry
A smile crept across your face
While I-
Got lost in the depth of your eyes
I hoped to keep my heart beat
Steadfast, at a synchronous pace
The sky swirled reminiscent to a Galaxy
I blinked to focus
Nina's "I'm going to put a spell on you"
Played in close proximity
Simply because -
Your scent teased me
As I laid in your shirt
Swept away by the blues
Of a love subdued

"But I do Love You"

"I don't like to be alone at night
And I don't like to hear I'm wrong when I'm right
And I don't like to have the rain on my shoes
But I do love you"

I used to sing that to you every night
Before we turned out the lights
And It was true
I did love you

But how does love like this manifest itself into something great?
It was like a blessing and you were the perfect mate
You seemed to be the person for me
Your sweet nothings were tunes that matched my melody

I'd do anything for you
Travel the world and build sand dunes with you
You were the king to my empire
Everything about you-
Kept me inspired.

Showed my rare shine similar to an eclipse
With you I thought I couldn't get any higher-
So I continue on with this harmony for you

"I don't like to be alone at night
And I don't like to hear I'm wrong when I'm right
And I don't like to have the rain on my shoes
But I do love you

Oh, I do love you"

Lust, Love, Loss

"Intrigued"

I knew it was something about you
When I looked in your eyes
The way my heart palpitated
At the sight of you.
How you'd brush my face so subtly
And trace my knee to the tune playing through your fingertips
The way in which you elevate me to a new level
My eyes locked on your lips
Your baritone articulated such vocabulary
It made the real
Become
Imaginary

"Tequila Sunrise"

Glistened the pearliness of water
Tangerine oranges
Kissed my hips
Resting on my skin
My melanin radiated

Tequila sunrise
The wind sung to me
Lullabies
Grounded me with the earth
To rest my racing mind

I can breathe again

Lust, Love, Loss

"Courage Finds Itself"

Courage finds itself
From a place from deep within,
I thought I had all the courage in the world, til I
Met you.
You see your skin was that radiated melanin
That kept women side eyeing
And grinning
Your stature stood firm and grounded
Your shoulders back
Confidence interlaced within every muscle
Courage found itself
In you
As it so graciously
MANifested

"HAZE"

A cloudy haze
Seemingly promotes distortion
Of thoughts
However, when I look at you
My focus is streamlined
I forget about my problems
You are indeed a gem
One that teaches me patience
Keeps me sane
You clear my haze
And calm my rage
Seemingly promoting clarity
Of thoughts

"Congestion"

Full of good and bad
The little things that make you wanna
Laugh.
The bigger things that capture your attention
Although, are you clever enough not to forget
The mention?
Of minute details-
You see
Through words and chaotic clues
You piece together the mystery
Deciphering the factual
From the actual
Memories we created in union
Cry!
Joy.
Pain.
Sunshine.
Rain.
Dry your eyes-
For the puddle reflects
Everything we've ever wanted answers
To
Instead we chose to...
DEFLECT

Lust, Love, Loss

"Woman as Mate"

Stand alongside not behind him
    Nurture his spirit and encourage him
Challenge intellect to stimulate his creativity
    Empower reflection to build and grow
Keep moments intimate, avoid outside opinions
    Unity, hand in hand forever more.

"You Are"

My love.
You are indeed a silent killer.
A force to be reckoned with.
When I look deep within-
I see,
All you are.
From your smallest smirk to chunky eyes.
And that sexy ass dimple-
On your left side.
You are remarkable.
It may take some time to see.
Don't give up!
'Cause after the tsunami-
Your ship will sail to sea.
You'll get to tell your story.
You won't be bogged down-
In sadness.
Caused by natural disasters.
You will rise from the tsunami.
In your humblest armor.
You have a gift!
You'll one-day share with us
Just seek to understand
You are a God.

Lust, Love, Loss

"When Love"

When love conquers all.

It is something that can't be explained.

No matter what, it's the defining line.

It's the first, last, and only thing that may keep the wheels turning in a relationship.

It will fuel the ups and downs and in between.

When love conquers all its the one thing we hold onto when everything seems to be gone...

When love conquers all in the end it shows us it is them and ONLY them

I long for from the beginning.

When love conquers all I'll always forever Love You!

Lust, Love, Loss

Loss

This acronym is sewn so intricately into us as we connect on various levels in society. Whether man, woman, adult, or child, we have all experienced this innate feeling. A feeling in the pit of our stomachs for when you feel as if you were holding weights. A place that usually resonates with darkness. Is it a lack of understanding as to why we feel the way we feel, how certain events have occurred in our lives, and what we could have done to prevent them. The language of finding the right words to say to console a loved one, friend, or even a stranger.

In this time, we must muster up strength such that we can pick up the pieces and carry on after these dark moments have caused uproars. Could it be that the reason it is so hard to keep the strength is because we generally can't take the good with the bad?

However, without the bad we cannot truly appreciate what is good. We must suffer to learn how to grieve properly rather than attempt to ignore our pain because it inevitably caused more damage.

In living, I find many of us are afraid of undergoing pain. Nonetheless, if we think about it as a mindset, then we can train ourselves to become accustomed and it will begin not to matter.

Pain is mind over matter. While everything else is matter over mind. It only matters if you mind.

We've trained our minds to normalize this feeling. How do we address what we have conditioned ourselves to feel? How we communicate verbal, physically, mentally, and emotionally attributes to how LOSS takes a toll on us.

Some age.
Some cry.
Some harm.
Some lie.

In the end, we all meet again because we all die.

Therefore, the Language of Suffering Souls (LOSS) is one that we will all endure but remember in that instant, the feeling is only temporary even when it seems the season is for an eternity.

Remember this too shall pass.

Unforgettably yours,

Mystkue

Table of Contents

Lust, Love, Loss

"My Daddy"

My daddy was a woman beater

But she didn't care as long as he didn't cheat her
She valued that hit
Like it was a twist of that good kush
On some cloud nine, Heroine-ish

After every episode
She'd still move with such grace
Pleading things, like
He's just sick
He's really a kind man
He's not cruel.
Just sick!

She believed so much in his lies
Her nightly cries became uniform
As he......
Mutilated her pretty face
Leaving battle scars
Some verbal, without a trace.

Those cries became her lullabies
I remember like it was yesterday

Until one night she stopped putting up a fight
Her lungs collapsed
Causing a vein to bust
And people always say

Lust, Love, Loss

Death don't come from heart ache and mistrust

I watched him
As he watched the spirit from her eyes disintegrate
He placed his peace sign
Over her like it was his final goodbye

Ironically,
He simply smiled and said until next time

Then he took a dramatic pause

Kissed her forehead
Thanked her even
I continued to watch him, conflicted and confused
I watched him kill my mother then thank her

I saw him kill my mother
The one who loved him like no other
I pondered. . . Why did he thank her?
It wasn't until his stature blocked my light
My bulb went off
Remember I said. . .

My daddy was a woman beater
He thanked her cause I was next
Back then was when I was 5
You can celebrate
'Cause I just turned 30
I survived.

"Roses I Didn't Send"

Send roses when they can smell them
I never did that for you
But I screamed,
I hollered,
Why?

When they told me you had closed your eyes.
Indefinitely!

An outflow of emotions came roaring
I never expressed how I felt about you.
Or your importance
Now here I am empty,
Trying to reconnect to you

On the day I said my final farewell
Two funerals-
Internally I died inside.
While your soul was soaring

The pain I felt without you
It's turbulent
My heart roaring

I should've
Sent roses when you could smell them
What I'd kill for another moment
Just to look at you

For every rose I didn't send you
I'll pick a petal and confess to you

Lust, Love, Loss

"Rejection"

Simply put more ways than one,
It scars!
Hits you like heavy tides-
Dragging deeper and deeper,
Into the abyss.

Unconsciously on this wild wave
Garnishing your emotional vulnerability
Keeping your feelings on guard
Always anxious.
No peace-
Or tranquility.

Would you think falling in love would be this hard?
Sleepless nights contemplating the why.
You aren't or will never be enough.
Realizing you weren't me to be their ace.

As the door slams shut
There was no love there
A slap in your face
Could you both communicate?
Resuscitate.
What once was?
Any sign of hello or goodbye
It scars.
Suppresses you internally,
Like drowning.

Simply put more ways than one

"Fell"

I took this the night I fell in love with you.
The night you lifted my chin,
And subtly gave me the keys to your world.
You see, you thought I fell in love with the things you could give me.
But no-

I fell in love with the innate
How you masterminded the equation of me
To which I hadn't yet recollected that there was a calculation.
Can you believe my frustration?
When I figured out that you reunited me
With me.

How you single handedly with your scholarly language
Read me like a book and told me that I had no clue what my real name
is
I fell in love with how you explained that I was the sum of two
Beings with a history
Yet somehow one was missing a variable
That left the family dynamic-
Equally unbalanced
What a mystery!

That missing integer which I later learned entered her
Was the man I once called father
Yes baby! I fell in love with you

Lust, Love, Loss

Simply because you were a symbol
That held his place

There was more to you than just that
I thought you had more meaning because you were my artist
You sculpted my way of thinking
Entertained my creativity and became my muse
Electrified me, aware of the intricate ways you blew my fuse

This is us now and that was us then
The night I fell in love with you
I'd do it all over again

"Shot Taker"

The shot taker is never the winner
He who gets the extra mile
Expectations explored in the eyes of a sinner

If she is what generates happiness
Then the ties that are bonds
Run deep through affection
Making this journey go from simple to steep

He must decide
What obstacles he can defeat
Is his goal to win-
Rather than be fulfilled?

Either way,
There's only one shot!

"Steelo"

You send chills down my spine, blood through my veins, you're an
extra beat in my heart!
That's what he said
He didn't mean it though
But it sounded good
Those words rolled off his tongue
So effortlessly
He was fluid
Like rivers
Flowing over rocks
Caressing your ego

Your tinted glasses
Blinded one fact
That was just
His steelo

Girl you thought!
You were,
The extra beat in his heart
Honey little did you know
The pulse
You fell for
Was a reaction
To his natural attraction.

You didn't take the time
To specify
Blood through my veins
Girl that line
You know the one

You send chills down my spine, blood through my veins, you're an
extra beat in my heart!

Should've sent you hella signs
Love had you amaurotic
So dim, you were just too blind
To see
That was just

His Steelo

"Contemplated"

I once contemplated suicide
Denied my happiness and peace of thoughts and mind
They did this to me
I carried no substance just as flat as my lifeline

Denied my happiness and peace of thoughts and mind
I didn't understand my soul or the importance of me
I carried no substance just as flat as my lifeline
To some extent have you ever, contemplated suicide?

I didn't understand my soul or the importance of me
No changes seemed to occur
To some extent have you ever, contemplated suicide?
My only friends were depression and anger

No changes seemed to occur
I once contemplated suicide
My only friends were depression and anger
They did this to me

"Shit! I may need to Deliberate"

If I told you that I love you more than life itself
Would you believe me?
OR
Would you question? How did I become this way?
For Christ's sake all this because I asked
You to-
Stay.
Arguments and debates
Is this a relationship?
Shit! I may need to deliberate
You may be just too much,
For me.
Not physically,
But mentally, spiritually
On my plate.

I want to feed your heart.
The nutrients it needs to pump.
Don't fuss and fight with me.
Cause I defend the fact I was never
Did I say never?
A quick hump!

Don't fuss and fight
Arguments and debates
Shit-
You may need to deliberate

I may just be too much
For you
Yes physically,
AND mentally, spiritually
On your plate.

Damn!
And I thought you could be that of a gentleman
But yet I just focused on the lust
Pressed up against-
-Between-
In sync with
The creases of our inseams
We were each other's
Adrenaline

If you told me, you loved me more than life itself
I would believe you
No second-guess
No question for you
I'd watched how you became that way
For Christ's sake that's why I asked
You to Stay.

"Losing"

The thought of losing you is demolition to my spirit.
You see, I'm so wrapped into you-
I make up the I D in your identity!
Without me, your incomplete.
Cause you and I,
We make up one entity.
You still trying to get rid of me?
When I bleed, you scream!
You trying to see eye to eye
One could try to start from the beginning or even the end
Inevitably we're still one.
Like palindromes-
The thought of losing you is demolition to my spirit.
Without you I feel invaluable.
Without me, there's no you.
You see, I make up the I D.
Without me,
You're a loss entity

Lust, Love, Loss

" "
.

Plagued by depression
Submerged with euphoria
The inner essence of me
Begins to implode

I bled for seven days
Which felt like eternity
Nights sweats and terrifying shivers

Still I felt less of a woman

I reminisced of a greater time
When you ushered me
And I screamed
Raymond
I second guessed myself
Attempting to connect the dots of blurred lines
Dreams vs Reality

Still I felt less of a woman

I fell into a gorge
Loathing in my pitfall
Alexithymia
I suffered silently

This occurred
Month after month
Time after time
Like poison in my mind

Still I felt less of a woman

My intuition sought clarity
Staring back at me
In this mirror of misery
I called reflection

At some point
It was time to take charge
To revisit
The little girl lost
To love her
Like no other

So, my spirit wouldn't crush
And what is unsaid
Was an understanding
That I was enough

Staring back at me
In this mirror of serenity
Is whom I love

A statuesque form
Secreting dope-ness
From my pores
The woman I've become
I've grown to adore

I am now more than ever... WOMAN.

Lust, Love, Loss

"Progression"

We say our exes are our exes for a reason.
Let it be lessons you learned helped you grow
Why let history repeat itself in a new season?
Don't be the ex,
Trying to screw over the next-
Cause you emotionally attached.
For this clandestine will bring you to an all-time low.
You see.
Your ex, might just hurt the next-
With the revelations of y'all meetings
Whether it's the secrecy or even the frequency
You must know they more inclined to make up before they break up
You see you the ex
And when it was y'all time,
Did you both put forth the effort to try your best
It's apparent that you had break up
Cause there was no more for either party to gain, if you made up
That's why-
We say our exes are our exes for a reason
You're not their scapegoat or justification for treason.

"Rights to Us"

The level of frustration injected the rhythmic pulse of your heart just
cause you never
Wanted-
Them to be right.
But they were right, and it pissed you off to your core
To say the least...

How could you deem yourself as so independent and buckle at the idea
of them, not being around?
Your blood rose, as you became distraught...
You contemplated if the cause was more ways than one your fault but
then you realized

You had told them that they were your muse
It was them- who had enough spark left
To light your fuse
They said you require much more
You obliged nonchalantly

The injected frustration of your rhythmic pulse kicked in
Cause you never wanted them to be right
You questioned
Were you worth it?
Were they?
Would they try to give you everything?
Would either subdue?
Without putting up a fight.

Lust, Love, Loss

Author's Thoughts

Thank you to every being known to man who broke my heart, gave me the feeling of doubt, or caused pain. You ignited my fire to write through my emotions. I let the pen bleed most times as I scribbled blindly, not collecting my thoughts to make a point until my heart felt soothed. My favorite poem in the loss series is "." The many emotions we as human beings go through and how they make us react always fascinates me. Loss feels like an emptying frame. Where we had something, there's a hole to which nothing present or foreseeable will be able to fill the space. Yet, loss also invites an ability to birth new things. What have you created because of loss?

YOUR LEGACY

_____

_____

_____

_____

_____

_____

_____

_____

_____

_____

_____

_____

YOUR LEGACY CONTINUED...

YOUR LEGACY CONTINUED...

Lust, Love, Loss

"Ain't that Fucked Up"

Girl you thought you were on cloud nine
The news-
Blunt force trauma to your skull
Your thoughts Columbined

You hear "he good, he got a girlfriend"
From the same guy who he once despised
The one he thought was too close
Da one that blurred the lines

Damn girl you was so clueless
Getting your heart broken simultaneously by 2 men
Now reflect on how you define
The word
Friend

Numb ain't the word
Got you frozen in motion
How could you be so foolish
Trying to understand how you fell under a spell
How effortlessly "let it go" departed from his lips

You question,
Which one of them was he referring to
What kind of woman are you?
That you ended up in this mess

Lust, Love, Loss

When ya ex left you for the unknown reason
And your next tell you he needed you for a season
But you coincidentally fell in love with both of these niggas
Shit, you somehow wish you could take back

Sis next time -
Don't ignore the signs
When the next tells you that him and the ex
Are one in the same
Don't be surprised by the congestion of tears
Forming in the corner of your eye lids

So now what
Cause you stuck on stupid
At first you thought it was the ex
But you realize it was both
They are one in the same

You the newest accessory of their similarities'
Low key, yeah! you the one to blame
You got that witchcraft love
And you sipped your own potion

Ain't that fucked up
Babygirl you slowly dying from within
All this-
All you wanted was unconditional love in the end

You wasn't enough either way
And you gave your Best

Lust, Love, Loss

You can say it, claim it
They lied.
They never loved you.
Sis, you was never different than all the REST.

But here's 1 more
A plan executed perfectly
Wrapped just right
Just so you'd receive it through your love language

.

.

Here's a poem "I wrote for you"
I see the future
I wonder what's next
I begin to unpack the word
I subtract the n and then the t
Guess what?
Now I too am ya ex!

Happy 25th!

Ain't that fucked up?

"Waves"

You need to treat me like you know!
I'm the waves in your ocean

Flowing free and fluidly
Brushing rippling, over barriers
Like the blood in veins, the Red Sea

Flowing free and fluidly

Over sand beds, all those bad things you've done to me
There simply memories

Flowing free and fluidly

"Mechanic"

Ties unravel or can be cut
Projection is only prevalent
Through reflection
Affection runs just as fast as
The speed of light
If he is the maker and the mechanic
Can he afford the upkeep?
The mechanic needs a support
Not to apply pressure
But be a backbone of force
One promise must be that the mechanic
Must not
Abort

"Having Everything Revealed"

Commiserating memories makes SHE the enemy
Fallen imagery; false depictions of HER
Reflections of past ignite one's misery
Growth within HER sheds dishonesty; trust
Every fallen petal writes HER legacy
Nightmares eradicated from a concrete rose

"Arrest"

Life just weighs heavy on this clenched fist.
A river of red runs rapidly over rocks, through it.
Its flow goes through canals and capsizes vessels.
A silent kill caused by outburst or elevated levels.
Oxygen acts as its ventilation.
And sometimes a thing called love
Causes suffocation
So much put -
On this clenched fist.
The central powerhouse.
The bane of one's existence.

Lust, Love, Loss

"Observation"

I can see your hesitation
Your lack of expression
You seemed disengaged
From that intimate
Level of
Compassion

"Perception"

To believe in the action without the word
Coerced by movement, sprinkled with emotions.
Acceptance of verbal neglect guided by fear.
Rejection
Abandoned in space with little to no strength.
Gravitational force infiltrates all seams within
Breaking, unraveling, diminishing...
Existence fades.
Time
There it is
Guilt
From a fallen soldier

"How"

How did I get into this mess
Never thought these would be issues I had to address
June 14, 2013
I asked her to be my girl
Man, oh man was I in for a thrill
Our relationship was blissful
For we both needed someone to love
And wanted to be love
I was Eric Benet and she Tamia
We'd look into each other's eyes
Singing spend my life with you

She taught me things about myself no one else could
She believed in me even when I didn't
And I should
There were things about her that she shared
And I tucked my thoughts away
Pretended I didn't care
She was scarred before I met her
She carried the bruises on her heart
That were sewn into her sleeve
It wasn't my plan to peel back the stitching
I wasn't even into fixing
Her
Issues
For I had my own

2 years had gone past and I noticed
She became impatient
You see she was a visionary
Like Picasso
She painted the mural of her life
Like a foreshadow of a movie
And I was just a struggling artist
But me
Sketching as I went along
Leaving signs of blurred lines
Waiting patiently for my next punchline
In all of this she decided to still stand tall
Still painting scenarios of our life together
In the market,
Overseas,
With our kids,
I mean she really planned forever
Our views some time intertwined through the kaleidoscope of our love
It was crazy we were in sync
I knew I loved her
And that would never go extinct

Another 2 years passed
Her patience had deteriorated
We both loved effortlessly
And that when things became too deep
Fighting not because we didn't love
But because she was consumed by me
And I had lost myself in us
She didn't know who I was more than I did

And then there were her mood swings
One day I was making her happy
And the next moment
I wasn't given her enough
I'd try to navigate these discussions in my mind
To say I wasn't ready
I her mind
She just wasn't enough

After trial and tribulations
Pondering and indecisiveness
I ended it
4.5 years later
I had learned so much and grown
But accidentally tainted her paint brush

Turbulence was in the air
And the Leary feeling I felt
As her words cut
Slaughtering
My masculinity
Had me feeling like
All this time
I had been
Neglecting me
But she knew just what to say
To mend the bruise and cover my heart
As darkness settled
Loneliness penetrated
Her venom

Pouring through the screen of my phone

Everyday I prayed silently
My love for her wouldn't go away quietly
I wanted nothing but her
At her best
She was a visionary
She deserved the extra-ordinary

So again
I ask
How did I end up in this mess
Here is where I confess

I'm a man and yes do I love her
But I've rocked the boat
Bringing someone new
To keep me afloat
I've kept it honest as I wanted my love
To be my homie
My friend

Our distance kept things still
And then I fucked up
I longed for us to talk
I needed you to have
That closure discussion
But that only led to
Consistent touching

If I could freeze that moment
I could replay it over and over again
Instead of pleading with her
It was my last time
Sliding in

Regret was not here
Just concepts
Right and wrong

You see she knew all along
That I may one day end up singing this song
Her question
. . .
Why did you bring someone else on board
When you know
I know
We jump ship
Climb aboard
Jump ship
Cause it keeps us afloat

Now I've deserted
Her in secret
And the one I claim to love
I'm mistreating

I just wanted the best for her
Didn't want anyone to steer her wrong
All along

The woman I loved
Succumbed to the title of second
To the one
I deserted
On the ship wreck

So how did I get myself into this mess?

"Giving"

Flooding him with gifts
Won't buy his love girls
You betta' off taking a few flicks
To remind
Of the early mornings
You were his balanced breakfast
Silly girls,
Don't you remember?
Trix!
Are for kids!
But that's what you get
Taking this journey passed your level
No cheat sheet
Although it's pretty fabricated
Like Candy-land
Love ain't no joke!
You couldn't even blink
Before you skipped a beat
Game over, only the strong are left to stand.
So, girls make a choice
Don't lose yourself in a river full of sweet nothings
Bottomless promises
When all you truly wanted was a couple of forevers
The one who finds you
Won't be a fool
Searching for
Gold.

"Just"

This door has revolved so many times
You'd think by now I'd come out,
Revolutionized!
But I'm still the same.
Humph, same old K.
Consistently playing misses fix it
Choosing to rearrange puzzle pieces
As the shit on my plate steadily increases.
But some might say, K
You thrive under pressure!
But can I ask a question,
Why is it you entrust me with your demons?
It's as if you've been told I have some type of gift
I can't purify you, I'm no cleanser
I'm just the ordinary misfit.
In this arrangement somehow, I've become a piece of the puzzle
Shape shifting to be to picture perfect
Better yet-
A work of art, like the light at the end of a tunnel.

But the confusion lies in place of the solution.
You can't solve anything without understanding.
Understanding
Entirely of the variables and their relations
In any situation.
But yet you managed to call on K,
To restore your satisfaction

And here I come subconsciously
Recreating the display of puzzle pieces
Arranging them to please, trying to find resolutions
But have you answered this question?
Why is it you entrust me with your demons?
It's as if you've been told I have some type of gift
I can't purify you, I'm no cleanser
I'm just the ordinary misfit.

"Did You Know?"

Did you know that every time he searched your eyes
While he pushed deep
That his emotions passion and lust was equivalent to her
For every time he traced his finger tip down your spine
Your hands grasped to cover more surface
Cotton
Polyester
Satin
As you braced for smooth impact
He thought of you as her

He only understood the similar love language he shared with her
With you
Craving of possessive feelings
Proving your worth to him
Asking for time via a clock who hands couldn't unwind
Separate
Disintegrate
A Ménage a trois unbeknownst to you that existed
Co-starring you
For every soft connection within each curve
HER

Your identity was a reflection of another
For all the things you projected
Marriage
House

Lust, Love, Loss

Dog

Children

His capability of taking you to ecstasy

Lead you here

Had you any clue?

This little game called life

Was a game of cat and mouse with her

And

Excluded the other woman (you)?

"Mom Mom's Tears"

Strength comforts you when we feel like the world is closing in on you.

Your tears will fill the ocean-

With the oxygen it needs to keep the ecosystem Alive.

Fear not that the pain you feel

Is simply the rhythmic vibration of the ocean floor

The shift of tectonic plates.

Causes memories to appear

You reminisce.

Your younger days were great!

The strength of the tear drop as it hits the shoreline will forever

Resonate!

In the waters-

Straight to HEAVEN as it restores your sorrow with love through

A spring shower and thunderous winter

Smile bright as you cry Dear

'Cause everything is going to be alright

The world isn't closing in on you it's simply-

Rotating on its axis to show you the awakening of a Brighter day!

Let your tears for where they may!

For everything whether dawn or dusk we be okay.

Lust, Love, Loss

"Go"

If you can't be what I need you to be
Then you must
Go
If you can't or not willing to be who I need
Then you must
Go

This doesn't take strategy
Not spades
So, stop counting the ways you can break
My heart

If you can't be what I need to be
If you can't continuously say you love me again and again
Then I'll be Toni D. Braxton and
Let it flow
If you can't be what I need you to be
If I can't make you happy
In other words, you should simply
Trust

This doesn't take strategy
I don't want to be
Just 4 play and lust
If you think I can't be what you need me to be
Then you
Must
You get the drift

Lust, Love, Loss

Shifting gears
What is your end goal in this?
Situationship
If I become contactless
If we can't be what we both need to be
Then we must
Go

Our separate ways

"If You Say You See Me"

If you say you see me
Then how come I was
Invisible as air
Standing in front of you?
We were miles apart
And I was lying next to you

But you see me

You're worried about me
You say
But you spend so much time
Speaking over me
You neglect to hear my thoughts
Whether verbally or emotionally
You mute me

You care
Then how come your glare

Is winters breath
Freezing me
And your hugs
Seem meaningless

But you see me?

Tensions are high
Our conflict never dies
Loving you seems to be
Steady warfare
Why we are enemies
Is unclear

Is it me misunderstanding
The depth of you
And whom you chose to be
Could I have become
Visually impaired
After hurting you

Creating miles between
The sheets
As you lay next to me
Suffocating your presence
Right in front of me

Have I lost sight of the initial engagement

Can I see you?

Lust, Love, Loss

"The Devil was an Angel"

The enemy lies in darkness
Dawned in Godly locs
Rooted from Cacao seeds
A painted masterpiece

Embodying strength like Kratos
Disguising his spirit of Hades
Enticing the interest of his prey
Showing her the fruits of labor
A glimpse of real love in her favor
Trickled with treats of chocolate

Tricks of his trade
An ensnare mastermind
Encapsulated the joker's spirit
To make her smile

He evoked fear
Stripping her close relationships,
Friendships
She relied on him
He was her savior

He praised her soul
Secretly premeditating
Larceny of her breaths
In the night

Seducing her before she slept
Breaking her spiritually
Torturing her through
Pleasure

Encapsulated the joker's spirit
To make her smile
He was a glimpse of real love in her favor
Trickled with treats of chocolate
He left her
Sightless
Breathless
Speechless

Strangling her Independence
Her confidence dangled delicately
Fluttering to the floor
Like rose petals

Life-less

The Devil was an Angel

Lust, Love, Loss

YOUR LEGACY

_____

_____

_____

_____

_____

_____

_____

_____

_____

_____

_____

_____

_____

_____

_____

_____

_____

_____

_____

_____

_____

_____

_____

_____

_____

_____

_____

_____

_____

_____

Lust, Love, Loss

Lust, Love, Loss

Lust, Love, Loss

Lust, Love, Loss

About Mystkue

Mystkue, pronounced mystique, just as the name defines, she exudes power and mystery in her tone and overall aura of the up and coming author. A native of Philadelphia, Mystkue began her journey of writing odes to love and sensual romance stories at the age of 14. Her characters portray such in-depth intrapersonal relationships with themselves that they connect their experiences with each and every one of her readers. Lust, Love and Loss is the second creative work by the upcoming author and poet.

"Your Petal Is Your Legacy"

Unforgettably Yours,

-Mystkue

Lust, Love, Loss

www.ingramcontent.com/pod-product-compliance
Lightning Source LLC
Chambersburg PA
CBHW020917090426
42736CB00008B/679